To the children of Mexico, Canada, and the United States
—B.R.

In memory of Homero Gómez González,
guardián of the monarchs,
and for all the people in the sanctuaries in Mexico
fighting today to preserve them for future generations
—E.M.

THIS IS A BORZOI BOOK PUBLISHED BY ALFRED A. KNOPF

Text copyright © 2022 by Barb Rosenstock
Jacket art and interior illustrations copyright © 2022 by Erika Meza

Visit us on the Web! rhcbooks.com
Educators and librarians, for a variety of teaching tools, visit us at RHTeachersLibrarians.com

Library of Congress Cataloging-in-Publication Data is available upon request.
ISBN 978-1-9848-2956-6 (trade) | ISBN 978-1-9848-2957-3 (lib. bdg.) | ISBN 978-1-9848-2958-0 (ebook)

The text of this book is set in 14-point Baskerville.
The illustrations were created using acrylic gouache, watercolor, ink, coffee splashes,
and pastel pencils, before using Photoshop to tie it all up.
Book design by Sarah Hokanson

MANUFACTURED IN CHINA
May 2022   10 9 8 7 6   First Edition
Random House Children's Books supports the First Amendment and celebrates the right to read.

THE MYSTERY OF THE MONARCHS

How Kids, Teachers, and Butterfly Fans Helped
Fred and Norah Urquhart Track the Great Monarch Migration

By

BARB ROSENSTOCK

Illustrated by

ERIKA MEZA

Alfred A. Knopf 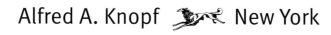 New York

Fred Urquhart ate breakfast, grabbed his satchel, and started his walk to school.

Thank goodness he stopped at the marsh.

Fred tramped through reeds, listened to crickets sing, and watched grasshoppers leap. He couldn't ignore that buzzing marsh in his Toronto neighborhood any more than a butterfly could ignore a sweet flower. By the time he was eight, Fred Urquhart was a bug man.

As the years flew, he gathered specimens for his insect collections. He studied biology and natural history. One day, Fred read an article written by a famous professor about migrating butterflies.

It made him wonder about *his* favorite butterfly, the monarch. Fred knew the monarch's life cycle: egg, larva, pupa, adult. He knew it needed the milkweed plant to survive. He knew that during the fall, the monarchs disappeared.

Fred wrote the professor. He asked:

WHERE DO THE MONARCHS GO?

He got a surprise answer: No one knew.

Butterfly experts agreed that monarchs arrived north in spring and vanished before winter. Some thought the monarchs flew off and died. Some thought they hibernated in or under logs. The professor thought monarch butterflies migrated to a warmer place.

But no one had ever seen
millions of monarchs in winter.
It was a mystery. Fred wanted
to solve it.

He studied entomology—bug science—at university, then worked at a museum and started tracking monarchs. He decided to catch monarchs, mark their wings, and let them go. Fred thought everyone was as curious about monarchs as he was. He expected other people to notice the marked wings and get in touch with him.

He stamped some monarchs with a number and made patterns of dots on others. He sprayed clusters of butterflies with oil paint. What a mess!

He made a tag with red ink numbers. It washed away.

Fred tried an addressed paper tag that he licked like a stamp. It fell off.

He created a gummed tag that stuck to itself through a tiny hole punched in the monarch's wing. This didn't hurt the butterflies and worked a bit better.

Fred tagged for ten years, but never got many back, and had no idea where the monarchs spent the winter.

Thank goodness he married Norah Patterson.

Norah loved Fred and his butterflies. As a team, they raised vegetables, chickens, a son, and thousands of monarchs for migration experiments at home.

Fred taught at a university. Later, Norah worked there, too. They developed a lighter, numbered, waterproof tag that read: **SEND TO ZOOLOGY UNIVERSITY TORONTO CANADA**.

It folded over the edge of the front right wing and didn't bother the monarchs one bit.

Two people could not tag enough butterflies to track millions. Fred asked other entomologists for help—not one responded. So Norah wrote about their project in a magazine and asked the public to tag monarchs.

Twelve people wrote back. Norah mailed off tags and instructions. These people began tagging monarchs. Then the Urquharts asked for help in newspaper articles. More people tagged and started returning any tagged monarchs they found to Fred and Norah. Some mailed the butterflies alive, packed in wildflowers. Other times Norah opened a box and discovered a tagged wing inside—the rest of the butterfly had been eaten by a wasp or a spider.

Fred put up a big map of North America. He and Norah plotted lines
with string from the spot a monarch was tagged to the spot it was recovered.

Farmers, librarians, truckers, and doctors joined the Urquharts'
"Insect Migration Association." Fred and Norah called their members
"Research Associates" and sent updates on monarch science. Regular
people acted as scientists—gathering tagging data, performing
experiments, and sending their findings to the Urquharts.

Who helped the most? Kids and teachers. Hundreds of classes joined Fred and Norah's research team. Third graders in Minnesota. Fifth graders in Iowa. High schoolers in Oklahoma. Capturing. Tagging. Releasing. Girls won prizes at science fairs. Boys raised money for research. Teachers brought caterpillars and chrysalides to school. All those kids and teachers asked: WHERE DO THE MONARCHS GO?

It was still a mystery.

One year, 13,800 monarchs were tagged and 128 were returned. The next, 17,000 were tagged and 298 returned. Fred, Norah, and their "butterfly family" were getting closer to an answer. Year by year, monarch by monarch, the lines on Fred and Norah's map pointed farther south. Ontario to Alabama, Indiana to Mississippi, New York to Florida.

Fred and Norah searched from the Atlantic to the Gulf of Mexico for a place millions of monarchs might hide. The lines on the monarch map gathered toward Texas. Norah and Fred hunted the valleys and hills from Brownsville to Big Bend. They watched flitting orange clouds headed up, up, and followed the monarchs across the Rio Grande.

The Urquharts drove through Mexico's states from Coahuila to Jalisco. They wrote in Spanish to newspapers. Kids in San Luis Potosí and teachers in Guadalajara helped tag. Fred and Norah traveled tens of thousands of miles. They had people in most every province and state in three countries asking:

¿A DÓNDE VAN LAS MONARCAS? WHERE DO THE MONARCHS GO?

It was STILL a mystery.

Thank goodness Catalina and Ken joined Fred and Norah's butterfly family.

Catalina Aguado and Ken Brugger loved adventures and lived in Mexico.

For two years, Ken drove their motorcycle down dirt roads while Catalina asked farmers and families if they'd seen monarchs.

Local people told of rugged forests filled with monarchs, which arrived late in fall and left in early springtime. Ken and Catalina hiked the mountains west of Mexico City. On January 2, 1975, 10,000 feet up in the cool forest on Cerro Pelón, they found . . .

Monarchs, millions of them. Blanketing the bark of oyamel firs.
Packed wing to wing on branches like orange leaves.

Later, Catalina and Ken phoned the Urquharts in Toronto.

Fred and Norah wanted to keep the location secret. To protect it.
To see it for themselves.

The next year, led by Catalina, Ken, and local mountain guides, Fred and Norah stepped into a forest of mystery.

Stunned by the sight, Fred sat down on a log. A branch, sagging with butterflies, broke off next to him. As he looked at the fluttering monarchs, he noticed one with a tag folded over its front right wing. Almost fifty years after asking the question, now Fred knew for sure.

Where do the monarchs go?

Aquí. Here.

> *"Not the least of the mysteries is how such a fragile, wind-tossed scrap of life can find its way (only once!) across prairies, deserts, mountain valleys, even cities, to this remote pinpoint on the map of Mexico."* —Fred Urquhart, 1976

Author's Note

In central Mexico, communities of Indigenous and non-Indigenous-identified people knew all about the monarchs in their forests. They celebrated the arrival of the butterflies around the end of the harvest and the Day of the Dead in early November. But they had a different question: *Where did the monarchs come from?*

Finding the answers to the monarch migration took more than 4,000 amateur scientists, 300,000 tagged monarchs, 3,800 news articles in multiple languages, and forty years of scientific research. The Urquharts first shared the sites where monarchs spend the winter (overwintering) in their *Insect Migration Studies* newsletter of 1975. Articles in scientific journals and *National Geographic* followed.

The eastern population of North American monarchs undertakes one of the longest migrations on the planet, up to 3,000 miles. Unlike flocks of birds, the monarchs migrate one by one, though each weighs no more than a paper clip and has never made the trip into Mexico's transvolcanic mountains before.

Why there? Monarchs can't survive freezing winters; the microclimate of the overwintering sites is perfect. The monarchs cluster on tall trees like the oyamel fir and Montezuma pine, protected from wind, rain, and sporadic snowfall. There is fresh water to drink, yet these forests stay cool enough to keep the monarchs relatively inactive. They don't fly often or mate, saving the energy that they will need for their return trip.

Though exact locations can vary, twelve to fourteen major overwintering sites have been identified. Many are protected by the Mexican government as part of a federal bioreserve called the Reserva de Biosfera de la Mariposa Monarca (Monarch Butterfly Biosphere Reserve). UNESCO declared the biosphere a World Heritage Site in 2008.

Though not the focus of this book, another population of North American monarchs breeds in western states, including Oregon, Washington, Idaho, Arizona, and Nevada, and overwinters in coastal California.

Monarch butterflies are found in a number of places around the world but have been most plentiful in the Americas. Here, the native monarch and its migration are in grave danger. People spray chemicals on insect pests, which can accidentally kill monarchs, and they use herbicides on farm fields, which kills milkweed, the only plant monarch larvae can eat.

An estimated 165 million acres of North American monarch breeding habitat has been lost since 1996. Although monarch populations can increase and decrease year to year, overall migrating monarch populations have declined at least eighty percent in the last twenty years. Extreme weather due to climate change affects monarchs, and some illegal logging continues within the protected sites.

People can destroy the monarch migration, or people can save it. There are still mysteries to be solved. There are still questions to be answered. The monarchs need young scientists like you.

Norah and Fred Urquhart in the field. Image courtesy of Robin Urquhart.

"Those who have had a dream and have lived to see that dream come true will have some conception of my feelings when I first entered the Mexican forest and there, before my eyes, was the realization of a dream that had haunted me since I was sixteen." —Fred Urquhart, 1976

Illustrator's Note

I was born in Michoacán, Mexico, a state that has adopted the monarch butterfly as its symbol. It is part of the culture, landscape, and everyday life for the locals, particularly for the people of the Purépecha and Mazahua native communities. The yearly arrival of the butterflies to their forests was never a mystery to them. It simply was: they knew that, every winter, the monarchs would come.

Even before Fred Urquhart started his research, the local population had already baptized the butterflies as "the daughters of the sun." Their arrival coincided every year with the Day of the Dead, so it was believed that the butterflies were lending their wings to the souls who were coming back to visit their loved ones in the land of the living. This doesn't mean, however, that people worshiped them. There were so many, and seeing them was such a common occurrence, the locals would even include them in their diet as a delicacy!

When I started working on this book, I visited El Rosario, one of the largest sanctuaries in Michoacán. I wanted to sketch the forest, the trees, the plants, and the environment, to try to capture the sensation of being in the middle of a butterfly overwintering site. But I also wanted to speak to the tour guides, the taxi drivers, the vendors, and the members of the community, and listen to what they would like to share with you, the reader of this book. For them, scientists learning where the monarchs go to overwinter was a turning point in their lives. Whereas before they had lived off the land and forest—farming and herding livestock—they were now working with conservationists who made them aware of the uniqueness of this phenomenon, and who wanted to keep the monarchs thriving and coming back.

These communities are organized in an economical system called

Monarchs in Mexico on Cerro Pelón. Image courtesy of Pato Moreno.

ejidos, which started in the times of the Mexican Revolution. This is a model of land tenure in which the community decides how the land will be used and shares the earnings among its members. So, collectively, they stopped growing crops and turned acres of land into a forest to preserve the wintering home of the butterflies. The people now sustain themselves, as well as their conservation efforts, with the ticket sales from the sanctuary. The tour guides rotate their duties during the week, sometimes bringing visitors up the designated paths, and sometimes patrolling the sanctuary, ensuring nobody disturbs the butterflies or cuts down any trees in the forest. They have learned how to live in harmony with the monarchs.

And when visitors come, by spending money on their lodging, tickets, and meals, and by respecting the rules and customs of the people who protect these wonderful beings, they are taking part in their protection, too.

The Life Cycle of a Monarch Butterfly

Monarch life cycle photos courtesy of Journey North's volunteers.

Caterpillar (or Larva)

A very small caterpillar hatches. It eats its eggshell and then gnaws on milkweed leaves, the only food it will eat. As the caterpillar grows, it molts (sheds its skin). The intervals between molts are called instars. Monarch caterpillars go through five instars. By the fifth instar, a caterpillar is about 2,000 to 3,000 times bigger than the day it hatched. A monarch is a caterpillar for seven to seventeen days.

Egg

Female monarchs lay tiny white eggs only on milkweed plants. Each egg is about the size of the head of a pin. A monarch is an egg for three to five days.

Adult Butterfly

A monarch butterfly emerges from its chrysalis, usually in less than two minutes. The new butterfly pumps fluid into its wrinkled wings, which stiffen and dry before flying. A male monarch has a black spot on each hind wing. A female monarch has more dark scales over the veins in her wings, which makes the veins look wider. Adult monarchs drink the nectar of many flowering plants through a curled, straw-like proboscis. The adults fly, mate, and reproduce. During mating, the males fertilize the eggs that females carry. The females lay fertilized eggs one by one on milkweed, and the cycle starts over. A monarch is an adult for two weeks to eight months. (See Butterfly Generations on the next page.)

Chrysalis (or Pupa)

The mature caterpillar spins a silk button and attaches itself head-down to a twig or other object. In about twenty-four hours, the skin begins to split and falls away, forming a bright green chrysalis with gold spots. Inside, the body parts that were only useful to the caterpillar are dissolved, and the material in them is used to make some of the adult butterfly's body parts. As the days pass, the wing scales develop, and the orange and black monarch butterfly can be seen through the chrysalis skin. A monarch is a chrysalis for eight to fifteen days.

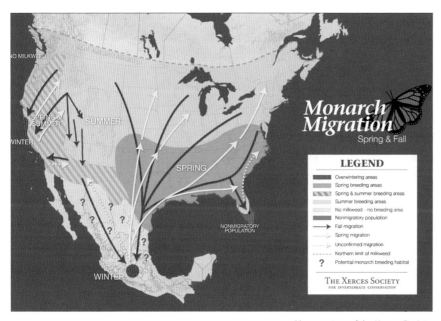

Map courtesy of the Xerces Society.

The Story of PS 397

On September 6, 1975, two junior high school students, Jim Street and Dean Boen, met their teacher, Jim Gilbert, to tag monarchs at the Minnesota Landscape Arboretum in Chaska, Minnesota. Mr. Gilbert had received numbered adhesive tags from Fred and Norah Urquhart. The boys and their teacher netted about 100 monarchs that morning. They placed tags onto the front right wings, then released the monarchs and sent their notes to the University of Toronto. One of the tags was numbered PS 397.

On January 18, 1976, Fred Urquhart reached into a pile of butterflies on Cerro Pelón, in the state of México, and picked up a monarch in good condition, with a tag numbered PS 397. That butterfly had been released five months earlier and 1,750 miles away in Minnesota, proving its migration. Two students and their teacher helped solve one of science's great mysteries.

Butterfly Generations

Three to four generations of the eastern population of North American monarchs are born in the spring and summer. These adult butterflies live for two to six weeks. But the last generation born in late summer is different. These adult butterflies will migrate as far as 3,000 miles to reach the mountains of central Mexico on the borders of the states of México and Michoacán. The monarchs in this last yearly generation do not reproduce on the way, and may live up to eight months in the overwintering areas of Mexico. When the overwintering generation begins to move back north in early spring, they lay the eggs that will become the first generation of a new year in the northern part of the monarchs' range.

Teacher Jim Gilbert and his students Dean Boen and Jim Street, courtesy of Jim Gilbert.

Dear Friend,

Beginning with Dr. Fred Urquhart's tagging program, our fascination with monarchs has inspired many monarch citizen science programs that continue today. The remarkable effort described in this book began a decades-long tradition for teachers, students, conservation advocates, and many others curious about monarchs and their habitat and migration. The tens of thousands of hours per year invested by these volunteers have helped us learn how and when monarchs use habitat, how their numbers change over time, and how monarch populations are responding to global change and conservation efforts. Fred and Norah were right: People *are* curious about monarchs and want to understand and save them. I hope that our conservation efforts will save enough monarchs for the migration to continue, and that we inspire enough people to answer the next big question: *How do the monarchs find their way?*

Our "butterfly family" is still growing, and monarchs need our help. Here are ways you can get involved: 1) Create habitat—in your yard, at your school, or at a local nature center. 2) Raise money to support local habitat conservation projects. 3) Join a monarch volunteer science project. See the information about Journey North on this page, or visit Monarch Joint Venture at monarchjointventure.org. 4) Tell everyone what you know about monarchs and how amazing they are!

K S Oberhauser

Karen S. Oberhauser, PhD

Director of the University of Wisconsin–Madison Arboretum
Co-founder and coordinator of the Monarch Larva Monitoring Project
Founding member and treasurer of the Monarch Butterfly Fund,
monarchconservation.org

Scientist Dr. Karen S. Oberhauser. Image courtesy of Karen S. Oberhauser, photo by Bryce Richter.

Journey North

Journey North is one of North America's premier citizen science programs for people of all ages. The project has over 60,000 registered sites in the United States, Canada, and Mexico—including teachers, schools, families, nature centers, and professional scientists. Reported sightings are mapped in real time as waves of migration move across the continent. To learn more about migration, ways to participate, educational materials, or how to donate, please visit journeynorth.org.

Symbolic Monarch Migration is a tri-national environmental education project that mimics the monarch migration. Young people across the United States and Canada create paper butterflies, which are shipped to young people in communities surrounding the monarch sanctuaries in Mexico. These "ambassador butterflies" adorn the walls of participating schools during the winter months. An environmental educator provides lessons to accompany these paper butterflies. The project is a partnership between Journey North and Monarchs Across Georgia, a committee of the nonprofit Environmental Education Alliance. To learn more, please visit eealliance.org/symbolic-migration.html.

Acknowledgments

My thanks to Dr. Karen S. Oberhauser, professor of entomology and director of the UW-Madison Arboretum, for her monarch expertise and enthusiasm for this project. Equal thanks to citizen scientist Don Davis, founding member and chair of the Monarch Butterfly Fund, for monarch science and tagging history. Fred and Norah's grandson, Robin Urquhart, and nephew, Lawrence Gulston, provided family photos and stories. Dr. Ellen Sharp and the people of Macheros, in central Mexico, educated me on local knowledge about monarchs. The book benefited from their review.

Selected Sources

Brower, Lincoln P. "Understanding and Misunderstanding the Migration of the Monarch Butterfly (Nymphalidae) in North America: 1857–1995." *Journal of the Lepidopterists' Society* 49, no. 4 (1995): 304–385.

Carson, Susan. "The Lost Kingdom of the Monarchs." *Ottawa Journal Weekend Magazine,* October 2, 1976, 13–14.

Dale, Daniel. "Couple's Home Was Butterfly Ground Zero." *Toronto Star,* April 18, 2009.

Monarch Watch, Urquhart Data. monarchwatch.org/tagmig/urq1.htm.

Oberhauser, Karen S., Kelly R. Nail, and Sonia Altizer, eds. *Monarchs in a Changing World: Biology and Conservation of an Iconic Butterfly.* Ithaca, NY: Cornell University Press, 2015.

Oberhauser, Karen S., and Michelle J. Solensky. *The Monarch Butterfly: Biology and Conservation.* Ithaca, NY: Cornell University Press, 2004.

Scott, Alec. "Where Do You Go, My Lovelies?" *University of Toronto Magazine,* August 24, 2015.

Slee, Mike (dir.). *Flight of the Butterflies.* DVD. Los Angeles: Shout! Factory, 2016.

Urquhart, F. A. *The Monarch Butterfly.* Toronto: University of Toronto Press, 1960.

Urquhart, F. A. "Monarch Migration Studies (An Autobiographical Account)." *News of the Lepidopterists' Society,* 4 (July/August 1978): 3–4.

Urquhart, F. A. "A Proposed Method for Marking Migrant Butterflies." *The Canadian Entomologist* 73, no. 2 (1941): 21–22.

Urquhart, F. A., and N. R. Urquhart. "Autumnal Migration Routes of the Eastern Population of the Monarch Butterfly (*Danaus plexippus L-Danaidae-Lepidoptera*) in North America to the Overwintering Site in the Neovolcanic Plateau of Mexico." *Canadian Journal of Zoology* 56, no. 8 (1978): 1759–1764.

Urquhart, F. A., and N. R. Urquhart. "The Overwintering Site of the Eastern Population of the Monarch Butterfly (*Danaus P. Plexippus;* Danaidae) in Southern Mexico." *Journal of the Lepidopterists' Society* 30, no. 3 (1976): 153–158.

Urquhart, Fred A. *The Monarch Butterfly: International Traveler.* Ellison Bay, WI: William Caxton Ltd., 1998.

Urquhart, Fred A. "Monarch Butterflies Found at Last: The Monarch's Winter Home." *National Geographic,* August 1976, reprinted at ncrcd.org /files/4514/1150/3938/Monarch_Butterflies_Found_at_Last_the_Monarchs _Winter_Home_-_article.pdf.

Urquhart, Fred A., and Norah Urquhart. *Insect Migration Studies Newsletter to Research Associates,* 1964–1994. Toronto: University of Toronto Press. Available at monarchwatch.org/read/articles/index.htm.

Urquhart, Frederick Albert. Oral History Interview, conducted by Paul A. Bator. 3 audio files. Toronto: University of Toronto Archives, January 8–12, 1979.

Williams, C. B. "Migrations of Butterflies." *Nature* 118 (July 24, 1926): 118–119.